WHY

Can't a computer do without 0s and 1s ?

AF516727

Om KIDZ

An imprint of Om Books International

Contents

Why is starting a computer called "booting up"?

It comes from the old expression "pulling up by your bootstraps" Your computer has a lot of work to do before it is actually ready to work. When you switch on the computer, it checks the RAM as well as information about drives in your computer. A memory chip called the BIOS chip (Basic Input/ Output System) stores all of this information. Once your computer has checked to make sure everything is working, it will display the desktop screen. This process of starting up is called 'booting up'.

Try this

Switch on your computer and note the time it takes to boot up.

Pocket fact

Boot Loader!
A boot loader is a computer program that loads an operating system or some other system software for the computer.

Why does my computer make funny noises when I turn it on?

It's because the hard drive has to start up! When you turn on the computer, the hard drive starts spinning the platters inside. This is what makes the whining sound that you hear at first. Then, there's a clicking sound as the hard drive moves the read/write heads back to the outer parts of the platter. These sounds are common and you usually hear them when you start your computer.

Why does a computer have a motherboard?

It is the main circuit board of the computer! The motherboard is a big board (usually green in colour) that connects all of the different parts of a computer including the CPU, memory and connectors for input and output devices. This lets all the parts of a computer work together.

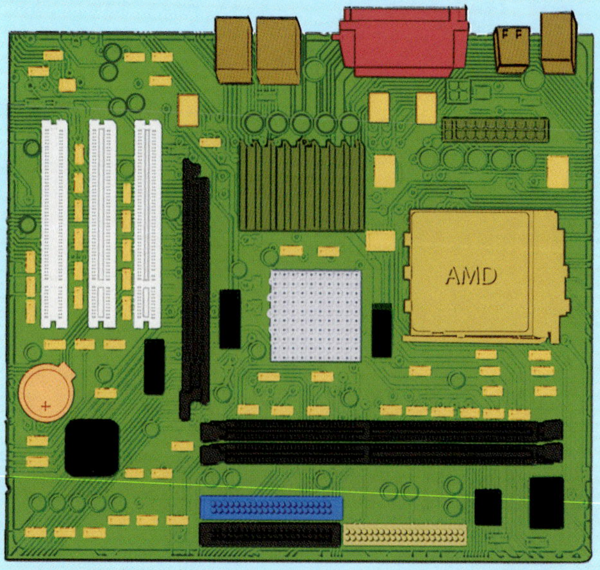

Pocket fact

The First Motherboard!

The first motherboard was released in 1981 and was used in the IBM Personal Computer. At that time, IBM referred to it as a "planar" instead of a motherboard.

Find out

What is a daughterboard?

Why are circuits in a computer so tiny?

So that the computers are of a portable size! The circuits in a computer are tiny because if the parts were larger, your computer would also be huge—maybe the size of your house and you couldn't have laptops or computer tablets! Also, the smaller you make computers, the faster they can go. By reducing the length of the wires and the distance between computer chips, you actually speed up the computer.

Why does a computer need a hard disk drive?

To permanently store and retrieve data on a computer! A hard drive is a secondary storage device that consists of one or more platters. Data is written on these platters using a magnetic head, all inside of an air-sealed casing. It is also where the computer's operating system, such as Windows or Linux is loaded.

Find out

What is a jump drive?

Pocket fact

The first hard disk drive!

The first hard drive was introduced by IBM on 13 September 1956. It had a storage capacity of 5 MB and a cost of about $50,000.

Why is the hard disk drive also called the C: drive?

Because it is the first available drive letter for hard drives! When personal computers were first invented they only had up to two floppy disk drives labelled A and B. Later, hard disks were added and were named drive C. As we install other drives, create new partitions, they will be assigned to other drive letters after C, such as D, E, F, G and so on.

Why are floppy disks called so?

They were quite fragile and tended to flop or hang loosely! A floppy or a floppy diskette is a type of storage device that can store electronic data, like a computer file. The original floppy disks were made out vinyl. These made the disks really flimsy and "floppy" hence they were named floppy disks.

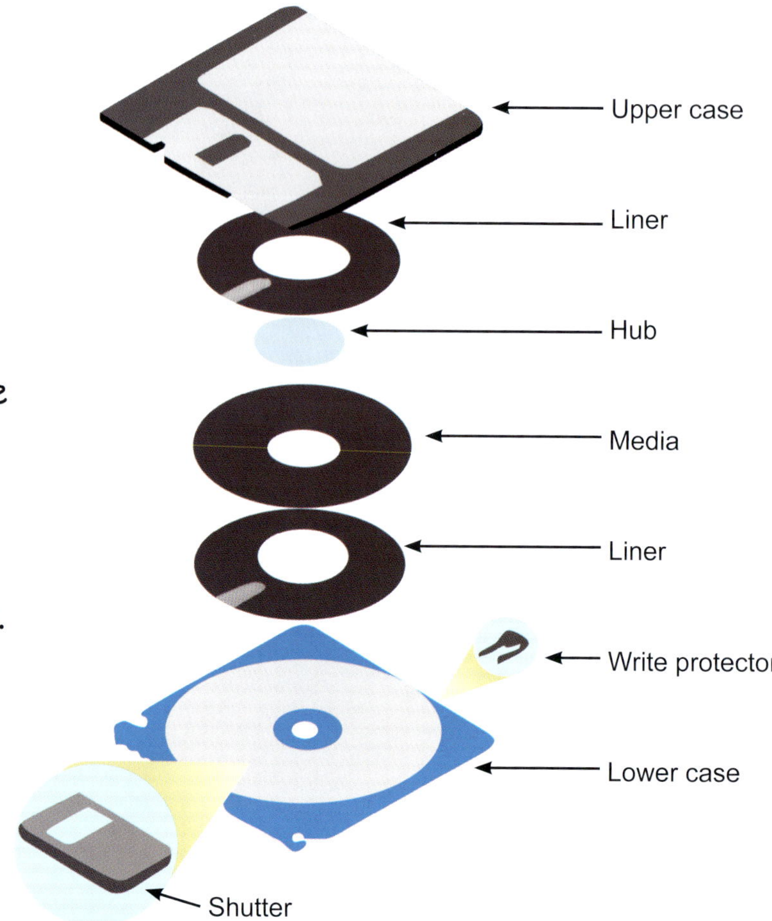

Find out

What was the size of the first floppy disks?

Pocket fact

The first floppy disk
The first floppy disk was released in 1971. It was invented by a team of researchers at the IBM.

Why don't we use floppy disks anymore?

We now work with much larger files! When floppy disks were introduced, the most common format was 1.44 MB. This could hold only very small amounts of data. Computers need a floppy drive to read floppy disks and modern computers are no longer supplied with a floppy disk drive because we now work with much larger files. We can now use CDs, DVDs, pen drives and zip drives to store these files.

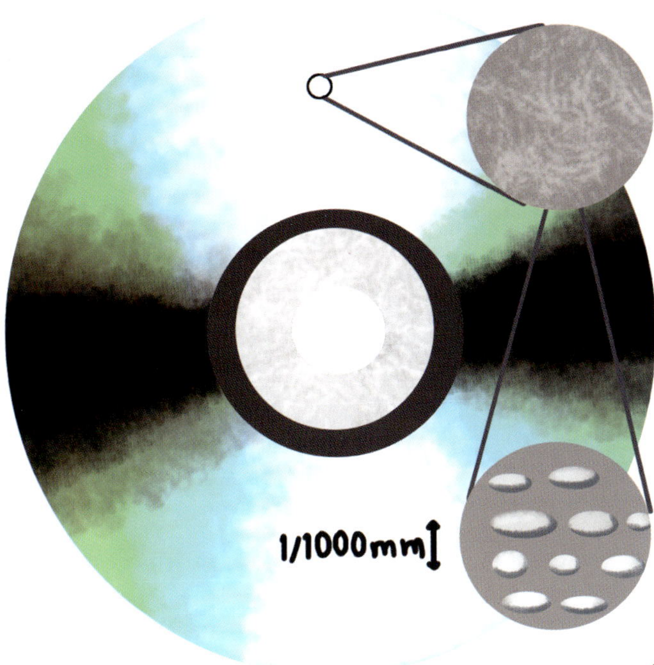

Why do CD-ROMs have little pits and scratches?

The pits are actually information! If you observe a CD-ROM with a microscope, you would see little pits and scratches on the compact disc. These pits are actually information! When the disc spins in the CD-ROM drive, a laser beam flashes on the pits and the computer reads the information off the disc.

Pocket fact

The first CD-ROM Format!
The CD-ROM format was first developed by the company Denon in 1982. It expanded on the Compact Disc Digital Audio (CDDA) format and created the CD-ROM format. This allowed it to store not only audio files but also other forms of data.

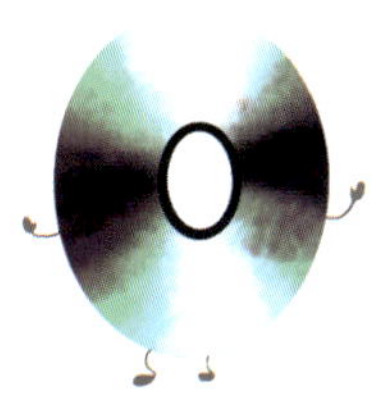

Find out

What is another name for a CD ROM Drive?

Why do we burn a CD or DVD?

Writing data to a CD or DVD is called burning it! When data is written to a CD or DVD, a laser is focussed at the surface of the disc to change the coating. This is called "burning" it. When the data is written, it is encoded in 0s and 1s. A darkened (burned) spot represents 0 and a translucent spot represents 1.

Why does a computer keyboard have function keys?

These keys act as shortcuts to certain functions! The function keys or f keys are lined along the top of the keyboard and labelled F1 through F12. These keys perform certain functions, like saving files or printing data. For example, the F1 key is often used as the default help key in many programs. The function of these keys differs according to the operating system and the software we use.

> **Find out**
>
> Where is the Fn key located on a laptop?

Why are there bumps on the F and J keys?

To help users correctly position their hands on the keyboard! You need to place your hands in an optimum position while typing on the computer. To help you with this, the F and J keys have bumps on them. The bump on the F key helps you place your left index finger and on the J key helps you place the right index finger!

> **Pocket fact**
>
> **Function Keys (f) and Function (Fn) key are different!**
> The Function (Fn) key is found on most laptops and some computers to perform special functions, such as turning up the screen's brightness and adjusting speaker volume. It is different from the f1 to f12 keys on a computer!

Why is a computer mouse called so?

The first computer mouse was given its name by its inventor, Douglas Engelbart. He called it so because its wire looked like the tail of a mouse. Initially the mouse was named "X-Y Position Indicator for a Display System". But this name was not popular and the mouse was instead called "turtle," which eventually became "rodent," and at last was renamed as "mouse."

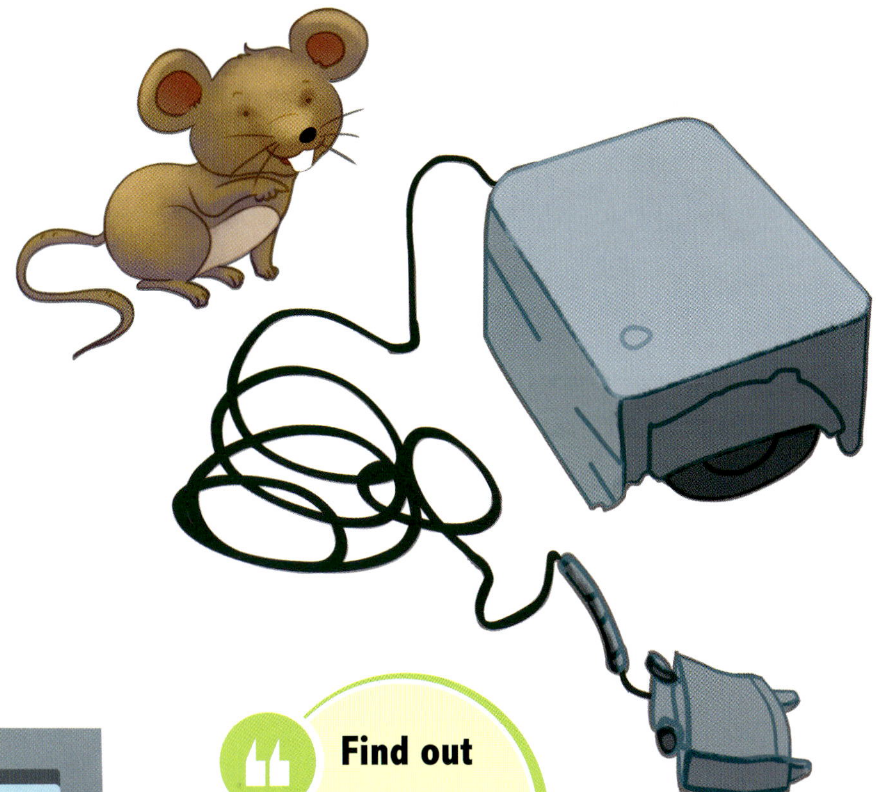

Find out

What is a spinning beach ball cursor?

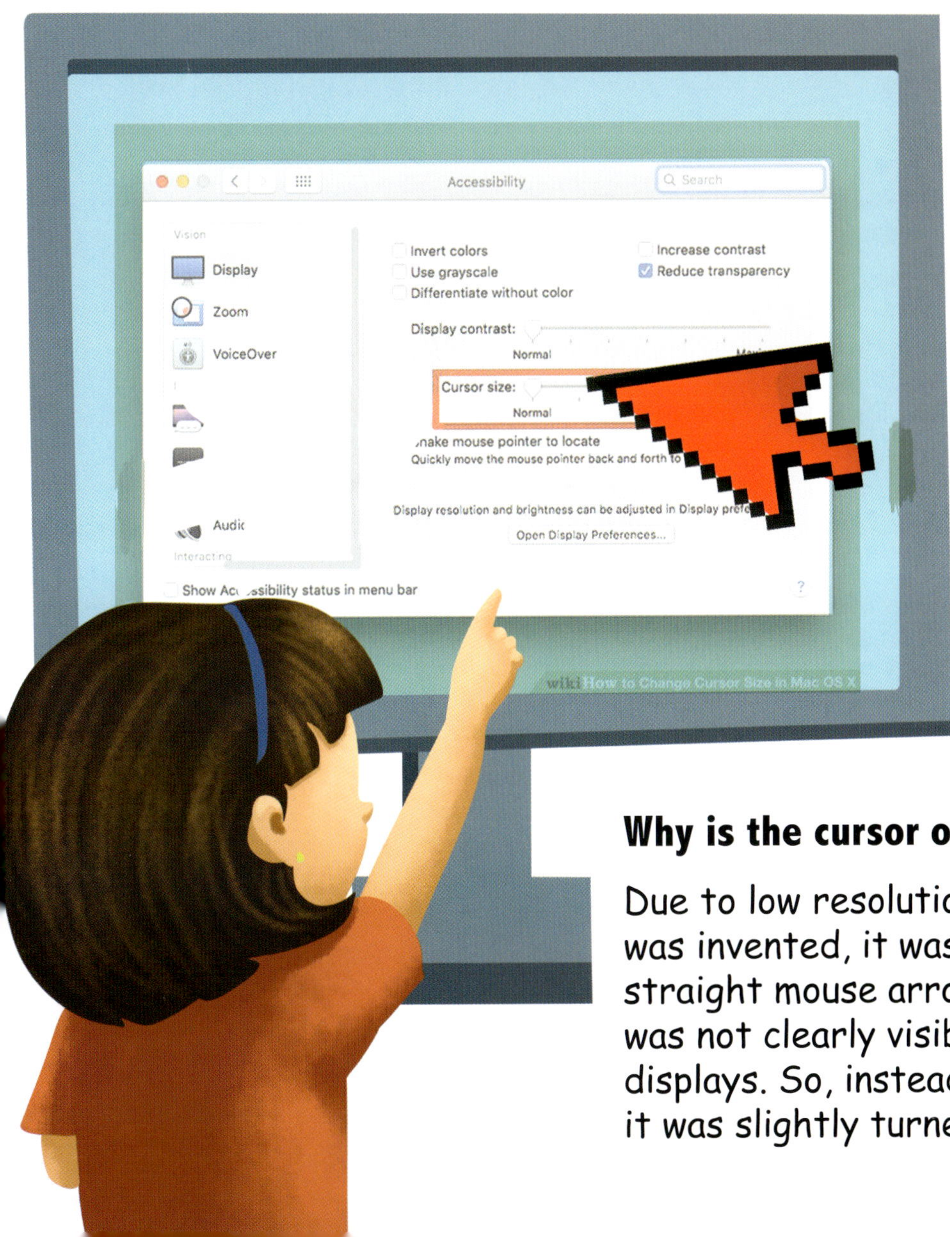

Pocket fact

The Windows Wait Cursor

The Windows wait cursor also called the hourglass cursor is a cursor that indicates that an application is busy performing an operation.

Why is the cursor of a mouse slightly tilted and not straight?

Due to low resolution displays! When the cursor of the mouse was invented, it was difficult for the developers to design a straight mouse arrow of small size. Also, the vertical arrow was not clearly visible to the users due to low resolution displays. So, instead of increasing the size of the pointer, it was slightly turned to 45° angle.

Why is software called so?

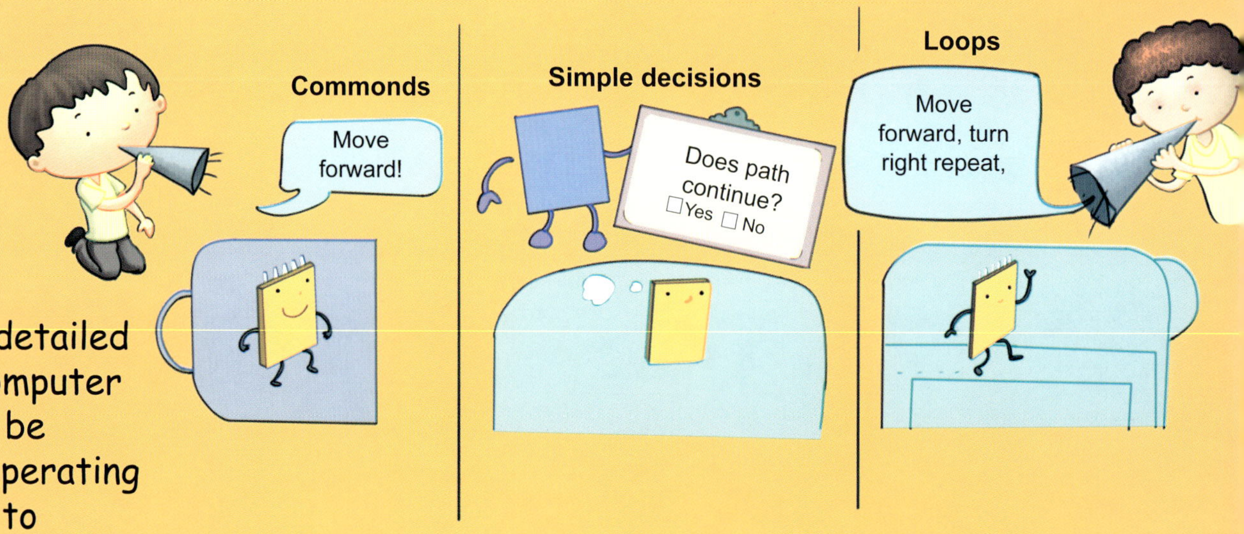

To distinguish it from hardware! Software is a program or a list of very detailed instructions telling the computer what to do. Software can be anything-from an entire operating system, such as Windows to a simple game. Hardware is something that you can touch, while software is information.

Find out

What does loading software mean?

Pocket fact

Interface Manager

The operating system Windows was first released in 1985. It was originally called Interface Manager.

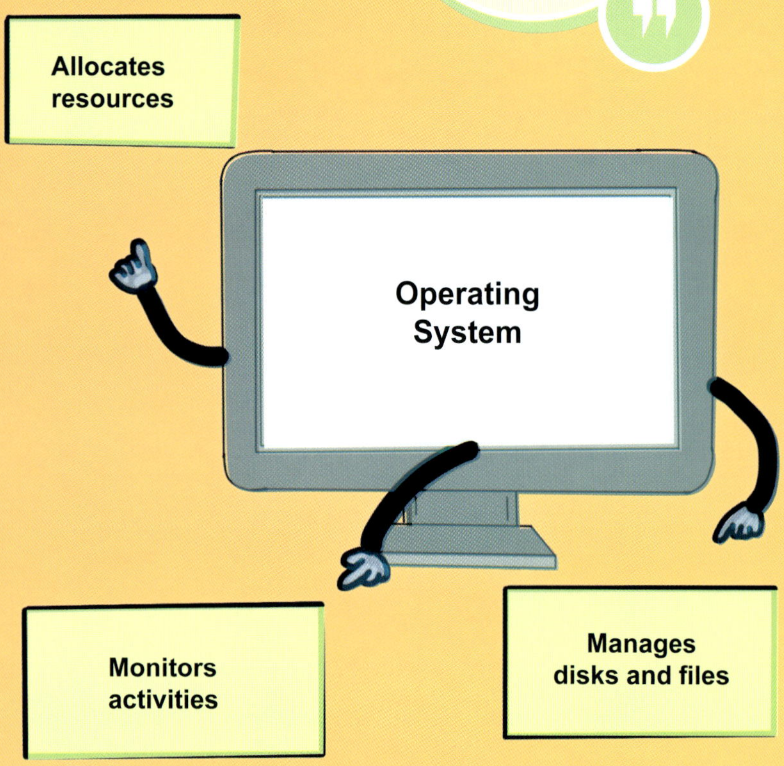

Why does a computer need an operating system?

It manages all of the software and hardware on the computer! An operating system is a software on the hard drive that enables the computer hardware to communicate and operate with the computer software. Without an operating system, a computer and software programs cannot be used.

Why does a computer need to restart after installing any software?

So that the installed software can come into effect! When a software is installed, it may require a DLL (Dynamic Link Library) file to be replaced. But it can't be done if the file is used by the operating system or any other application. So, we restart the computer after installing a software and the system is free to change the relevant files.

Pocket fact

Head Crash!
A head crash refers to the hard disk failure. It occurs when a read-write head of a hard disk drive comes in contact with its rotating platter. This results in permanent damage to the magnetic media on the platter surface.

Find out

What is a bug in computing?

Why do computers crash?

When there are bugs in the operating system! Crash is a word used to describe software and hardware failures that cause it. Sometimes when there are bugs or viruses in the software, they can cause problems with a computer's operating system. When the operating system has problems, the entire computer can freeze and crash.

Why can't a computer do without 0s and 1s?

These are the only numbers a computer understands! Computers don't have brain as humans. They just understand two states- off and on, which are represented by 0 and 1. Whatever instructions we give to the computer are converted into 0 and 1. The computer processes this information and gives us the result.

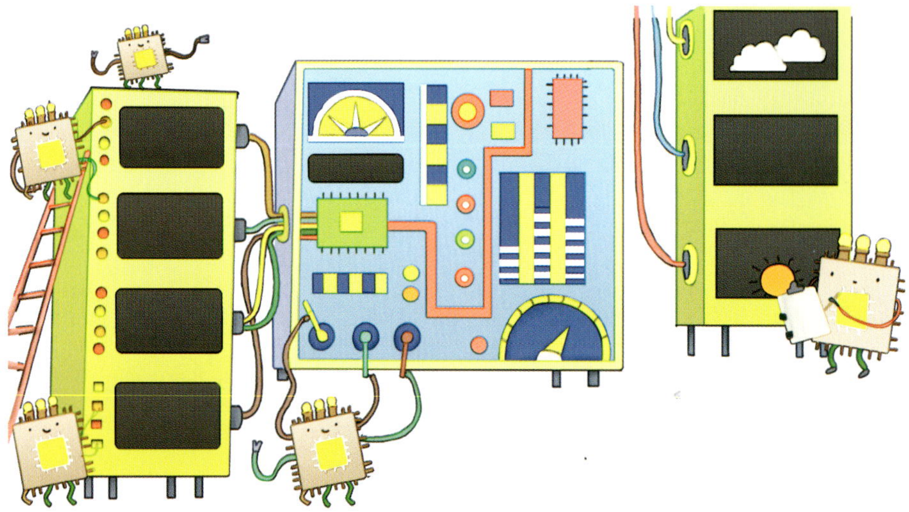

Find out

What is a computer clock cycle?

Pocket fact

Either 32-bit or 64-bit!

A computer with a 32-bit processor can only have a 32-bit version of an operating system installed. It cannot have a 64-bit version of an operating system installed.

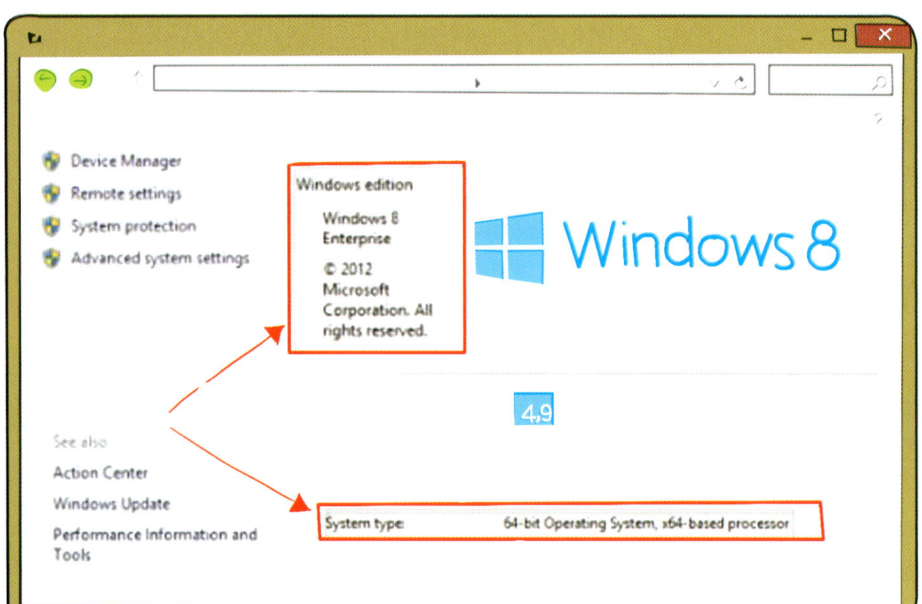

Why do computers have 32-bit and 64-bit operating systems?

It refers to the way a computer's processor, CPU handles information! 32-bit and 64-bit are types of CPU architecture that are capable of transferring bits of data per cycle. It is the amount of information your CPU can process each time it performs an operation. Computers with 64-bit operating system are faster than 32-bit operating systems.

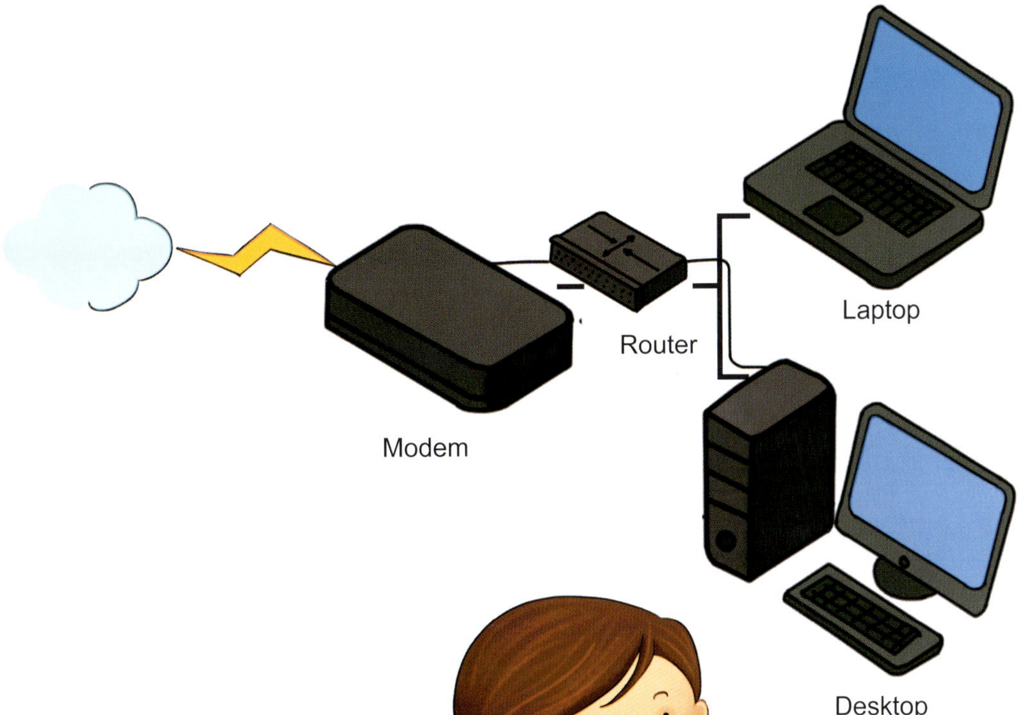

Why do we need a modem?

To help it communicate with other computers! A modem is a device that allows your computer to communicate with other computers through a telephone line. A telephone wire is attached from the modem to a telephone jack. The modem changes your data into sounds to send it through the telephone wires, and then another modem on the other end changes the sounds back into data.

Pocket fact

Dataphone!
The first Modem was known as the Dataphone. It was released by AT&T in 1960.

Find out

What is the full form of Modem?

Why are dial-up modems so noisy?

It is the sound of your modem communicating with another modem at the other end of the phone line! Modems originally sent data over a network that was designed to only carry voice. Because of that, the communication between two modems was in the hearing range else it would not get carried on the phone line. However, modern modems are not noisy because the phone system can now carry both voice and data at the same time (DSL).

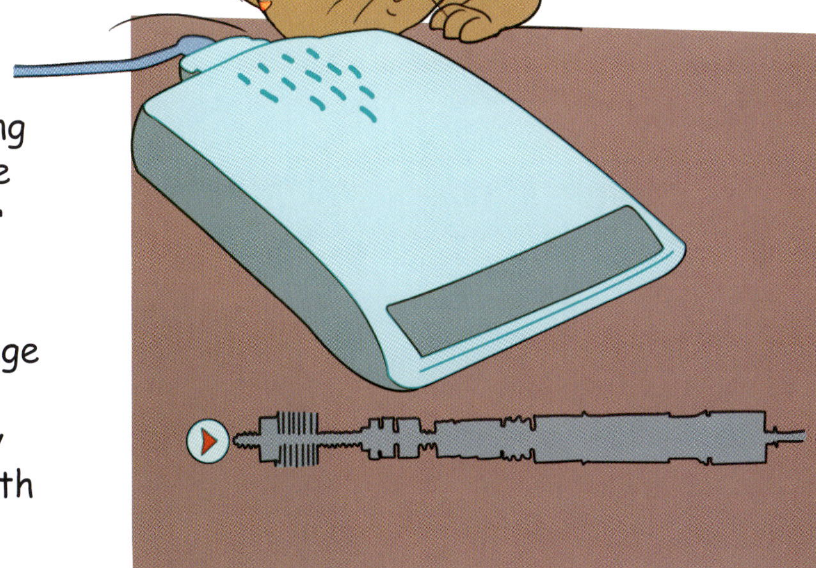

Why do different websites end in different extensions?

They help us identify different domain names on the Internet! The extensions at the end of website or domain names are called Internet domain suffixes. The **.com** tells the computer that you are looking for a commercial website. Addresses that end in **.gov** are government websites and those that end in **.edu** are colleges or universities.

Find out

What is a search engine?

Pocket fact

Scavenger hunt!

A scavenger hunt is an educational lesson which introduces the Internet to us. It is a tool that helps us follow clues to find things or guides us how to search the Internet.

Why does the Internet slow down sometimes?

There can be a number of reasons! The most common problem that slows down your Internet connection is malware, such as viruses, spyware and adware. Sometimes the fault lies with your Internet Service Provider, also known as your ISP. The ISP may experience technical difficulties from time to time. Routers and servers get overloaded and occasionally break down. When these problems arise, it often results in slow Internet connection.

Why do my parents turn on 'parental controls' on the online service?

To keep you safe on the Internet! All the online services have a feature called 'parental controls' that allows parents to keep children away from inappropriate and dangerous sites, restrict access by time. For example, no social media sites during homework time.

Find out

Who is a newbie?

Pocket fact

The First Spam
The first electronic spam mail was composed by Gary Thuerk. It was sent in 1978 as an advertising email to 393 recipients on ARPANET.

Why shouldn't we click on unknown links in emails?

They can be malware programs! Clicking a link in an email may not always be dangerous but we should be aware of the risks. Some emails contain links to download a malicious file such as a virus Trojan or malware. Such files can harm your computer or even steal your personal information.

Index